Lessons from the 2020 Operation Alba in Venezuela's Borders

Copyright Page

TITLE: Lessons from the 2020 Operation Alba in Venezuela's Borders

1ST Edition

Copyright @ 2023

ISBN: 9798223681007

Table of Contents

Lessons from the 2020 Operation Alba in Venezuela's Borders

By Roberto Miguel Rodriguez

Chapter 1: Operation Alba: The 2020 Multinational Peacekeeping Mission in Venezuela's Border Regions

Background of Operation Alba

Operation Alba, the 2020 multinational peacekeeping mission in Venezuela's border regions, was a significant response to the escalating security challenges and instability in the area. This subchapter explores the background and context that led to the establishment of Operation Alba, shedding light on the factors that necessitated such a multinational cooperation effort.

Venezuela's border regions had been plagued by violence, drug trafficking, and organized crime for years, creating a dire humanitarian situation for the local communities. The escalating conflict between criminal groups, along with the political and economic instability in the country, had severe consequences for the civilians living in the border regions. The United Nations (UN), recognizing the urgent need for intervention, played a crucial role in facilitating the formation of Operation Alba.

The UN's involvement in Operation Alba was instrumental in coordinating the efforts of various countries and non-governmental organizations (NGOs) to address the security challenges in the region. With its experience in peacekeeping missions and conflict resolution, the UN provided guidance and support to ensure the effectiveness and success of the operation.

One of the key objectives of Operation Alba was to deliver humanitarian aid to the affected communities. The mission aimed to alleviate the suffering of the civilians by providing them with essential supplies, medical assistance, and support services. The coordination and cooperation among the participating nations and NGOs were crucial in ensuring the efficient delivery of aid and maximizing its impact on the ground.

Multinational cooperation and coordination played a pivotal role in the success of Operation Alba. The participating countries pooled their resources, expertise, and personnel to tackle the security challenges collectively. This approach not only enhanced the effectiveness of the mission but also fostered greater understanding and cooperation among the nations involved.

Operation Alba also emphasized the importance of gender perspectives in peacekeeping operations. Efforts were made to ensure the participation and inclusion of women in decision-making processes and peace negotiations. Recognizing the unique experiences and vulnerabilities faced by women in conflict-affected areas, Operation Alba aimed to address their specific needs and promote gender equality.

Evaluating the effectiveness of Operation Alba in maintaining peace and stability was crucial to assessing its impact on the Venezuelan communities and civilians. This subchapter explores the various indicators and methodologies used to evaluate the mission's success, taking into account the complex nature of the conflict and the challenges faced on the ground.

Additionally, the subchapter delves into media coverage and public opinion of Operation Alba in Venezuela and internationally. The role of the media in shaping public perception and understanding of the mission, as well as the challenges and biases encountered in reporting, are examined.

In conclusion, this subchapter provides a comprehensive overview of the background and context of Operation Alba. It highlights the significance of multinational cooperation, the role of the United

Nations, the challenges faced in Venezuela's border regions, and the impact of the mission on the local communities. By examining various perspectives and dimensions, historians and other interested readers can gain a deeper understanding of this crucial peacekeeping effort.

Objectives and Mandate of Operation Alba

Operation Alba, the 2020 multinational peacekeeping mission in Venezuela's border regions, was established with specific objectives and a clear mandate. This subchapter aims to provide historians and interested readers with an in-depth understanding of the goals and responsibilities assigned to this critical mission.

The primary objective of Operation Alba was to promote peace and stability in Venezuela's border regions, which had been plagued by violence, insecurity, and instability. The mission sought to address the security challenges faced by these regions and restore a sense of normalcy for the local communities.

Under the mandate of the United Nations, Operation Alba had several key responsibilities. Firstly, it aimed to facilitate the delivery of humanitarian aid to the affected populations. This entailed ensuring the safe and efficient transportation of essential supplies, including food, medical aid, and shelter, to those in need.

Additionally, Operation Alba emphasized multinational cooperation and coordination in its peacekeeping efforts. It recognized that addressing the complex challenges in Venezuela's border regions required a collaborative approach, with various nations pooling their resources and expertise. The mission established mechanisms for effective coordination among participating countries, enabling them to work together towards common goals.

Operation Alba also prioritized the protection and support of Venezuelan communities and civilians. It recognized the importance of their involvement in the peace process, aiming to empower them and provide platforms for their voices to be heard. The mission emphasized engaging with local communities, understanding their needs, and implementing initiatives that would have a positive impact on their lives.

Furthermore, Operation Alba integrated gender perspectives into its peacekeeping operations. It recognized the importance of promoting gender equality and women's empowerment in conflict-affected areas. The mission sought to ensure the active participation of women in decision-making processes and address the unique challenges they face in post-conflict environments.

To evaluate the effectiveness of Operation Alba, various parameters were considered. These included the mission's ability to maintain peace and stability in the border regions, its impact on the local communities and civilians, and its ability to deliver humanitarian aid efficiently.

The subchapter also explores the role of non-governmental organizations (NGOs) in supporting Operation Alba. It highlights the crucial contributions made by these organizations in delivering aid, providing essential services, and promoting community resilience.

Finally, the subchapter discusses media coverage and public opinion of Operation Alba, both in Venezuela and internationally. It analyzes the role of the media in shaping public perception of the mission and its impact on public support for peacekeeping efforts.

In summary, this subchapter provides a comprehensive overview of the objectives and mandate of Operation Alba. It highlights the mission's commitment to peace, stability, humanitarian aid delivery, multilateral cooperation, and community engagement. By examining the different facets of this mission, historians and those interested in Operation Alba can gain a deeper understanding of its significance and impact on Venezuela's border regions.

Participating Countries in Operation Alba

Operation Alba, the 2020 multinational peacekeeping mission in Venezuela's border regions, saw the collaboration of several countries from around the world. The participating countries played a crucial role in addressing the security challenges, delivering humanitarian aid, and ensuring peace and stability in the region.

One of the key players in Operation Alba was the United Nations, which provided support and coordination to the mission. The UN's involvement was instrumental in bringing together countries with diverse interests and expertise to work towards a common goal. Its role in facilitating peace negotiation and diplomacy was crucial in resolving conflicts and maintaining stability.

Several countries participated in Operation Alba, contributing troops, resources, and expertise. The United States, as a major regional power, played a significant role in the mission, providing both military and logistical support. Other countries, such as Canada, France, Germany, and the United Kingdom, also played an active part in the operation, bringing their experience in peacekeeping and conflict resolution.

Non-governmental organizations (NGOs) also played a critical role in supporting Operation Alba. These organizations, with their expertise in humanitarian aid and development, worked alongside the participating countries to deliver much-needed assistance to the affected communities. Their presence ensured that the mission had a comprehensive approach, addressing not only security concerns but also the needs of the local population.

The participation of NGOs also brought attention to the gender perspectives in peacekeeping operations in Venezuela's border regions. They highlighted the importance of considering women's rights, empowerment, and protection in the mission's strategies. Recognizing the unique challenges faced by women and girls during times of conflict, efforts were made to ensure their inclusion and participation in decision-making processes.

Operation Alba had a direct impact on Venezuelan communities and civilians. The mission provided a sense of security and stability, allowing communities to rebuild and thrive. The delivery of humanitarian aid was crucial in addressing the immediate needs of the population, including access to healthcare, food, and clean water.

The effectiveness of Operation Alba in maintaining peace and stability is an important aspect to evaluate. Historians will analyze the mission's strategies, the cooperation and coordination among participating countries, and the impact on the local communities. The evaluation will provide valuable insights into the lessons learned and best practices for future multinational peacekeeping missions.

The media coverage and public opinion of Operation Alba, both in Venezuela and internationally, also played a significant role in shaping the mission's perception. The media's portrayal of the mission and its outcomes influenced public opinion and the level of support for the operation. Understanding the media's role in shaping public perception will contribute to a comprehensive analysis of Operation Alba.

In conclusion, the participation of various countries and organizations in Operation Alba demonstrated the importance of multinational cooperation in peacekeeping efforts. The mission's impact on Venezuelan communities, the strategies employed, and the evaluation of its effectiveness will provide valuable lessons for future peacekeeping missions. Through collaborative efforts, countries and organizations can work together to bring peace and stability to conflict-affected regions.

Chapter 2: Role of the United Nations in Operation Alba

UN's Peacekeeping Role in Conflict Zones

The United Nations (UN) has played a crucial role in maintaining peace and stability in conflict zones around the world. One such example is Operation Alba, a multinational peacekeeping mission conducted in Venezuela's border regions in 2020. This subchapter will delve into the UN's role in this operation, focusing on its strategies, challenges, and impact on the local communities.

The UN's involvement in Operation Alba was pivotal in coordinating and facilitating multinational cooperation in the peacekeeping efforts. As historians, it is important to understand the various dimensions of this operation and the role played by the UN. The organization's primary objective was to promote peace and stability in the conflict-ridden regions of Venezuela's borders.

In order to achieve this goal, the UN faced numerous security challenges and devised effective strategies to address them. These challenges included armed groups, drug trafficking, and illegal immigration. The UN worked closely with local authorities and other stakeholders to develop security measures and implement them effectively.

Operation Alba also witnessed the delivery of humanitarian aid to the affected communities. The UN played a crucial role in coordinating and facilitating this aid delivery, ensuring that it reached the people who needed it the most. This aspect of the operation highlights the UN's commitment to the well-being of the local population.

Multinational cooperation and coordination were essential components of Operation Alba. The UN worked closely with various countries and international organizations to ensure a unified and effective approach to peacekeeping efforts. This cooperation demonstrated the importance of collaboration in maintaining peace and stability in conflict zones.

The impact of Operation Alba on Venezuelan communities and civilians was significant. The mission provided a sense of security and hope to the affected population. The UN's efforts in facilitating peace negotiations and diplomacy were instrumental in resolving conflicts and fostering reconciliation.

Non-governmental organizations (NGOs) also played a crucial role in supporting Operation Alba. These organizations provided much-needed assistance in areas such as healthcare, education, and infrastructure development. The UN worked closely with these NGOs to ensure a comprehensive and sustainable approach to peacekeeping.

The gender perspective in peacekeeping operations was also a significant aspect of Operation Alba. The UN ensured the inclusion and participation of women in decision-making processes, recognizing their unique perspective and contributions.

Evaluating the effectiveness of Operation Alba in maintaining peace and stability is crucial for future peacekeeping efforts. This subchapter will explore the various metrics and indicators used to assess the success of the operation, considering both short-term and long-term outcomes.

Lastly, media coverage and public opinion of Operation Alba, both in Venezuela and internationally, played a significant role in shaping perceptions of the mission. This subchapter will analyze the media's portrayal of the operation and the public's perception of the UN's role in peacekeeping.

In conclusion, the UN's peacekeeping role in conflict zones, exemplified by Operation Alba, highlights the organization's dedication to maintaining peace and stability. This subchapter will provide historians with valuable insights into the UN's strategies, challenges, and impact in conflict zones, specifically in the context of Operation Alba and its lessons for future peacekeeping missions.

UN's Involvement in Operation Alba

The United Nations' involvement in Operation Alba, the 2020 multinational peacekeeping mission in Venezuela's border regions, played a crucial role in addressing the security challenges, delivering humanitarian aid, and maintaining peace and stability in the region. This subchapter explores the UN's role in this mission and its impact on Venezuelan communities and civilians.

The United Nations, as a global organization dedicated to maintaining international peace and security, played a significant role in Operation Alba. The UN's involvement was essential in coordinating and facilitating the multinational cooperation and coordination efforts among the participating countries. Through its peacekeeping department, the UN provided technical and logistical support, expertise, and guidance to ensure the smooth implementation of the mission.

In Operation Alba, the UN's primary focus was on the security challenges in Venezuela's border regions. The UN worked closely with the participating countries to develop effective strategies to address these challenges, including border control, disarmament, and demobilization efforts. The UN's presence and involvement helped create a secure environment for the delivery of humanitarian aid to the affected communities.

Humanitarian aid delivery was another crucial aspect of the UN's involvement in Operation Alba. The UN agencies, such as UNICEF and the World Food Programme, played a significant role in coordinating and delivering essential supplies, including food, water, and medical assistance, to the affected communities. The UN's expertise in humanitarian operations ensured that aid reached those in need efficiently and effectively.

Furthermore, the UN's involvement in Operation Alba also focused on peace negotiation and diplomacy. The UN acted as a mediator between the participating countries and the Venezuelan government, facilitating dialogue and negotiations to achieve a peaceful resolution. The UN's diplomatic efforts helped build trust among the parties involved and create a conducive environment for long-term peace and stability.

The UN's collaboration with non-governmental organizations (NGOs) was instrumental in supporting Operation Alba. NGOs provided additional resources, expertise, and assistance in areas such as human rights protection, gender perspectives, and community development. The UN's partnership with NGOs strengthened the overall effectiveness of the mission and ensured a comprehensive approach to peacekeeping and community support.

Lastly, the UN's involvement in Operation Alba had a significant impact on Venezuelan communities and civilians. The mission provided a sense of security and stability, allowing communities to rebuild and recover from the effects of violence and insecurity. The delivery of humanitarian aid improved living conditions and provided much-needed support to vulnerable populations. The UN's presence also helped foster trust and confidence in the international community, paving the way for future peacekeeping efforts.

In conclusion, the United Nations' involvement in Operation Alba was instrumental in addressing security challenges, delivering humanitarian aid, and maintaining peace and stability in Venezuela's border regions. The UN's coordination, expertise, and diplomatic efforts ensured the success of the mission and had a positive impact on Venezuelan communities and civilians. The UN's role in Operation Alba serves as a valuable lesson in multinational cooperation in peacekeeping efforts and highlights the importance of international organizations in promoting peace and stability in conflict-affected regions.

UN's Contributions to the Mission's Success

The success of Operation Alba, the multinational peacekeeping mission in Venezuela's border regions, can be attributed to the significant contributions of the United Nations (UN). The UN played a crucial role in various aspects of the mission, ensuring its effectiveness in maintaining peace and stability.

One of the primary contributions of the UN was its involvement in the coordination and cooperation among the participating nations. The UN acted as a mediator, facilitating dialogue and negotiation between different actors involved in the mission. Its diplomatic efforts helped to bridge differences and create a unified approach towards achieving the mission's objectives.

In addition, the UN played a vital role in ensuring the delivery of humanitarian aid in the conflict-affected areas. It coordinated with non-governmental organizations (NGOs) and other humanitarian actors to provide essential supplies, medical assistance, and support to the affected communities. The UN's expertise in humanitarian operations and its extensive network of partners were instrumental in overcoming logistical challenges and reaching those in need.

Furthermore, the UN brought a gender perspective to the peacekeeping operations in Venezuela's border regions. It emphasized the importance of promoting gender equality and women's empowerment in all aspects of the mission. The UN advocated for the participation of women in decision-making processes and worked towards addressing the specific needs and vulnerabilities of women and girls in the conflict-affected areas.

The UN's role in peace negotiation and diplomacy was also crucial to the success of Operation Alba. It facilitated dialogue between the conflicting parties and helped to build trust and consensus. The UN's expertise in conflict resolution and its neutrality as an international organization made it a trusted mediator in the peace process.

The contributions of the UN were not limited to the operational aspects of the mission. It also played a significant role in shaping public opinion and media coverage of Operation Alba, both in Venezuela and internationally. The UN's communication strategies effectively conveyed the mission's objectives and achievements, garnering support and understanding from the public.

Overall, the UN's contributions to the success of Operation Alba were invaluable. Its involvement in coordinating and cooperating among nations, delivering humanitarian aid, promoting gender equality, facilitating peace negotiations, and shaping public opinion played a vital role in maintaining peace and stability in Venezuela's border regions. The lessons learned from the UN's involvement in Operation Alba can serve as a valuable resource for future peacekeeping efforts.

Chapter 3: Security Challenges and Strategies in Venezuela's Border Regions

Political Instability and Conflict Dynamics in Venezuela

Political instability and conflict dynamics have long plagued Venezuela, creating a volatile environment that demands the attention of historians and scholars interested in understanding the intricacies of Operation Alba. This subchapter delves into the complexities of political instability and conflict dynamics in Venezuela, shedding light on the factors that have contributed to the need for a multinational peacekeeping mission.

Venezuela's political landscape has been marked by frequent shifts in power, with competing factions vying for control. The rise of Hugo Chávez in the late 1990s brought about a period of populist governance, characterized by increased state control over the economy and heightened political polarization. Chávez's policies, while popular among certain segments of the population, also exacerbated tensions and deepened divisions within Venezuelan society.

The subsequent presidency of Nicolás Maduro saw the country descend into further chaos. Economic mismanagement, rampant corruption, and a decline in democratic institutions fueled widespread discontent and led to mass protests. As the government cracked down on dissent, human rights violations became increasingly common, leading to an influx of refugees fleeing the country.

These internal dynamics, combined with external pressures and geopolitical interests, created a fertile ground for conflict in Venezuela's border regions. The presence of armed groups, drug trafficking networks, and cross-border criminal activities further destabilized the region, posing security challenges that required a multinational response.

Operation Alba, a multinational peacekeeping mission launched in 2020, aimed to address these challenges by promoting stability, security, and the protection of human rights in Venezuela's border regions. The United Nations played a crucial role in coordinating the efforts of the participating countries, ensuring a unified approach to peacekeeping.

The mission also relied on the support of non-governmental organizations (NGOs) to provide humanitarian aid and support to the affected communities. These organizations played a critical role in delivering much-needed assistance to vulnerable populations, particularly in the areas of healthcare, education, and food security.

Moreover, Operation Alba recognized the importance of gender perspectives in peacekeeping operations. Efforts were made to ensure the inclusion and participation of women in decision-making processes, as well as to address gender-based violence and promote gender equality within the mission.

The effectiveness of Operation Alba in maintaining peace and stability in Venezuela's border regions is an ongoing subject of evaluation. While progress has been made in certain areas, challenges persist, and the mission continues to adapt its strategies to address evolving dynamics on the ground.

The media coverage and public opinion of Operation Alba, both in Venezuela and internationally, have played a significant role in shaping perceptions of the mission. The dissemination of accurate information and the engagement of the public in the peacekeeping efforts are crucial for building trust and garnering support for the mission.

In conclusion, political instability and conflict dynamics in Venezuela have necessitated the deployment of a multinational peacekeeping mission. Operation Alba, with its focus on cooperation, coordination, and the protection of vulnerable populations, strives to bring stability and peace to Venezuela's border regions. However, the challenges faced by the mission are numerous, and ongoing evaluation is crucial to ensure its effectiveness and impact.

Security Threats in the Border Regions

The border regions of Venezuela have long been plagued by security threats, making them a challenging environment for peacekeeping operations. This subchapter will explore the various security threats that have been encountered during Operation Alba, the multinational peacekeeping mission that took place in 2020.

One of the primary security threats in the border regions is the presence of armed groups and criminal organizations. These groups, involved in drug trafficking, illegal mining, and other illicit activities, have created a volatile and unstable security situation. The peacekeeping forces involved in Operation Alba have had to navigate these complex dynamics, often facing direct confrontations with these armed groups.

Another significant security threat is the presence of cross-border violence and conflicts. Due to the porous nature of the borders, conflicts from neighboring countries often spill over into Venezuela, exacerbating the security situation. Operation Alba has had to address these conflicts and work towards de-escalation and resolution, often through diplomatic negotiations.

Additionally, the border regions are susceptible to the infiltration of terrorist organizations. These organizations take advantage of the weak governance and security infrastructure in these areas to establish their presence. Operation Alba has focused on intelligence gathering and cooperation with international partners to counter these threats and prevent any potential terrorist activities.

Furthermore, the border regions are susceptible to human trafficking and the smuggling of weapons and contraband. These activities not only pose security risks but also contribute to the erosion of the rule of law and the stability of the region. Operation Alba has collaborated with local law enforcement agencies to combat these illicit activities and strengthen border control measures.

Overall, the security threats in the border regions of Venezuela present significant challenges to peacekeeping efforts. Operation Alba has adopted a comprehensive approach, combining military operations, diplomatic negotiations, and cooperation with international partners to address these threats. However, the complexity and ever-evolving nature of the security situation require ongoing vigilance and adaptability.

This subchapter will provide a detailed analysis of the security threats faced during Operation Alba, examining the strategies employed to mitigate these threats and maintain peace and stability in the border regions. By understanding the security challenges encountered and the effectiveness of the peacekeeping efforts, historians can gain valuable insights into the complexities of multinational cooperation in peacekeeping missions.

Strategies Employed by Operation Alba to Address Security Challenges

In the face of mounting security challenges in Venezuela's border regions, Operation Alba implemented a range of strategies to effectively address and overcome these obstacles. This subchapter delves into the various tactics employed by the multinational peacekeeping mission to ensure the safety and stability of the region.

One of the primary strategies utilized by Operation Alba was the establishment of robust intelligence networks. Recognizing the importance of accurate and timely information, the mission prioritized the collection and analysis of intelligence to identify potential threats and respond proactively. This involved close collaboration with local communities, utilizing their knowledge and insights to gather vital intelligence on criminal organizations, smuggling routes, and other security risks.

Another key approach employed by Operation Alba was enhanced border control measures. Given the porous nature of Venezuela's borders, the mission focused on strengthening security checkpoints and increasing patrols to prevent illegal activities, such as drug trafficking and arms smuggling. By effectively monitoring and regulating border crossings, Operation Alba aimed to disrupt criminal networks and prevent the inflow of illicit goods.

Furthermore, the mission prioritized community engagement and collaboration. Operation Alba recognized that sustainable peacekeeping efforts required the cooperation and support of local communities. As such, they actively engaged with community leaders, civil society organizations, and local authorities to build trust and foster positive relationships. By involving local stakeholders in decision-making processes and incorporating their perspectives, Operation Alba ensured that security measures were tailored to the specific needs and concerns of the communities they served.

Additionally, Operation Alba placed a strong emphasis on comprehensive training programs for its peacekeeping personnel. Recognizing the complexity of the security challenges they faced, the mission provided specialized training on topics such as counter-terrorism, conflict resolution, and human rights. This enabled peacekeepers to effectively respond to a wide range of security threats while adhering to international standards and norms.

Overall, the strategies employed by Operation Alba in addressing security challenges in Venezuela's border regions were multifaceted and comprehensive. By establishing intelligence networks, enhancing border control measures, prioritizing community engagement, and providing rigorous training, the mission was able to effectively maintain peace and stability in the region. However, the effectiveness of these strategies and their long-term impact will require careful evaluation and analysis in order to draw meaningful lessons for future peacekeeping efforts.

Chapter 4: Humanitarian Aid Delivery in Operation Alba

Importance of Humanitarian Aid in Peacekeeping Missions

The Importance of Humanitarian Aid in Peacekeeping Missions

Humanitarian aid plays a crucial role in peacekeeping missions, and its significance cannot be overstated. In the context of Operation Alba, a multinational peacekeeping mission in Venezuela's border regions, the delivery of humanitarian aid has been instrumental in maintaining peace and stability, as well as supporting the local communities and civilians affected by the conflict.

One of the primary objectives of humanitarian aid in peacekeeping missions is to address the immediate needs of the affected population. In the case of Operation Alba, this includes providing food, clean water, medical supplies, and shelter to those displaced by the conflict. By meeting these basic needs, humanitarian aid helps alleviate the suffering of the local communities and fosters a sense of security and stability.

Moreover, humanitarian aid also serves as a tool for building trust and fostering cooperation between the peacekeeping forces and the local population. By demonstrating a genuine commitment to the well-being of the civilians, peacekeepers can establish a rapport with the community, which is essential for effective peacekeeping efforts. This trust-building process is especially critical in conflict zones where the local population may be wary of external interventions.

Additionally, humanitarian aid can contribute to long-term peacebuilding efforts by addressing the root causes of the conflict. By investing in infrastructure development and economic revitalization projects, humanitarian aid can help create opportunities for the local communities, thereby reducing the grievances and tensions that often fuel conflicts. Such initiatives can also promote reconciliation and social cohesion among different ethnic or religious groups, fostering a sustainable peace.

Furthermore, the delivery of humanitarian aid in peacekeeping missions is closely linked to the principles of international humanitarian law. It ensures the protection of civilians, particularly vulnerable groups such as women and children, from the atrocities of war. Humanitarian aid also upholds the principle of humanity, emphasizing the importance of preserving human dignity and alleviating suffering, irrespective of political or military considerations.

In conclusion, humanitarian aid plays a vital role in peacekeeping missions, and its importance in Operation Alba cannot be overstated. By addressing the immediate needs of the affected population, building trust and cooperation, contributing to long-term peacebuilding efforts, and upholding international humanitarian law, humanitarian aid serves as a catalyst for peace and stability in Venezuela's border regions. Its effective delivery and coordination are crucial for the success of Operation Alba and similar multinational peacekeeping missions worldwide.

Challenges in Delivering Aid in Venezuela's Border Regions

Introduction:

The delivery of humanitarian aid in Venezuela's border regions has been plagued by numerous challenges. Operation Alba, a multinational peacekeeping mission initiated in 2020, aimed to address these challenges and provide much-needed assistance to vulnerable communities. This subchapter will explore the various obstacles faced by humanitarian actors in delivering aid in Venezuela's border regions, shedding light on the complexities of operating in this volatile environment.

1. Security Challenges:

One of the major hurdles in aid delivery in Venezuela's border regions is the prevailing security situation. The presence of armed groups, drug cartels, and criminal networks has created an environment of violence and insecurity. Humanitarian actors often find themselves at risk of attacks, theft, and extortion, hampering their ability to deliver aid effectively. Strategies such as establishing secure transit corridors and coordinating with local security forces have been employed to mitigate these risks.

2. Access Constraints:

Venezuela's border regions are characterized by difficult terrain, including dense forests and impassable rivers. These geographical barriers pose significant challenges in reaching remote and isolated communities in need of aid. Additionally, bureaucratic hurdles, including restrictive government policies and checkpoints, often impede the timely and efficient delivery of humanitarian assistance.

3. Lack of Infrastructure:

The lack of basic infrastructure, such as roads, bridges, and healthcare facilities, further complicates aid delivery in Venezuela's border regions. Limited transportation networks make it difficult to transport large quantities of aid, resulting in delays and increased costs. Moreover, the absence of proper healthcare facilities hampers the delivery of medical assistance to communities in need.

4. Interference and Corruption:

Political interference and corruption present significant obstacles to aid delivery in Venezuela's border regions. Local authorities and armed groups may attempt to divert aid for their own benefit or create barriers to access. This necessitates close coordination with the United Nations and non-governmental organizations (NGOs) to ensure aid reaches its intended recipients.

5. Cultural and Linguistic Barriers:

Venezuela's border regions are home to diverse indigenous communities with distinct cultural and linguistic identities. Overcoming language barriers and understanding local customs and traditions is essential in ensuring aid delivery is sensitive and appropriate. Engaging with local community leaders and employing interpreters can enhance the effectiveness of humanitarian efforts.

Conclusion:

Delivering aid in Venezuela's border regions remains a formidable challenge due to security concerns, access constraints, lack of infrastructure, interference and corruption, as well as cultural and linguistic barriers. Operation Alba, in collaboration with the United Nations, NGOs, and local actors, has sought to address these challenges and bring much-needed relief to vulnerable communities. By understanding and addressing these obstacles, future peacekeeping missions can improve their effectiveness in maintaining peace, stability, and delivering humanitarian aid in similar contexts.

Successful Approaches to Humanitarian Aid Delivery in Operation Alba

In the context of Operation Alba, the successful delivery of humanitarian aid has been a crucial aspect in maintaining peace and stability in Venezuela's border regions. This subchapter aims to highlight the effective approaches and strategies employed by multinational forces and organizations in ensuring that humanitarian aid reaches the affected communities and civilians.

One of the key approaches to successful humanitarian aid delivery has been through the coordination and cooperation of various actors involved in Operation Alba. Multinational forces, non-governmental organizations (NGOs), and the United Nations (UN) have worked together to pool their resources, expertise, and networks to ensure efficient and timely delivery of aid. This collaborative approach has allowed for a comprehensive understanding of the needs on the ground and has facilitated a more targeted and effective response.

Another successful approach has been the establishment of secure and accessible transportation routes for aid delivery. Given the security challenges in Venezuela's border regions, ensuring the safety of aid convoys has been paramount. Multinational forces have worked to secure these routes, providing a protective presence and minimizing the risks of violence or interference. This has enabled aid to reach even the most remote and vulnerable communities.

Furthermore, the involvement of local communities and leaders in the aid delivery process has been crucial. Recognizing the importance of local knowledge and participation, Operation Alba has actively engaged with community leaders, civil society organizations, and grassroots initiatives. This approach has not only ensured that aid is targeted towards the most urgent needs but has also fostered a sense of ownership and empowerment within the affected communities.

In addition, gender perspectives have been integrated into the humanitarian aid delivery process. Recognizing the unique needs and vulnerabilities of women and girls, efforts have been made to provide gender-sensitive aid, including access to reproductive healthcare, gender-based violence support services, and economic opportunities. This inclusive approach has not only addressed the immediate needs of women and girls but has also contributed to their long-term empowerment and resilience.

Overall, the successful approaches to humanitarian aid delivery in Operation Alba have been characterized by coordination, collaboration, and a comprehensive understanding of the local context. By working together, securing transportation routes, involving local communities, and incorporating gender perspectives, Operation Alba has been able to effectively deliver aid to those in need, contributing to the maintenance of peace and stability in Venezuela's border regions.

Chapter 5: Multinational Cooperation and Coordination in Peacekeeping Efforts

Importance of Multinational Cooperation in Peacekeeping

The Importance of Multinational Cooperation in Peacekeeping

In today's complex and interconnected world, the importance of multinational cooperation in peacekeeping efforts cannot be overstated. The subchapter "Importance of Multinational Cooperation in Peacekeeping" explores the significance of collaboration among different nations and organizations in maintaining peace and stability, with a specific focus on Operation Alba, a multinational peacekeeping mission conducted in Venezuela's border regions in 2020.

Operation Alba: The 2020 Multinational Peacekeeping Mission in Venezuela's Border Regions

Operation Alba serves as a prime example of the vital role played by multinational cooperation in peacekeeping endeavors. This subchapter delves into the specifics of the mission, highlighting its objectives, composition, and the challenges faced by the multinational forces involved.

Role of the United Nations in Operation Alba

The United Nations played a crucial role in Operation Alba, providing the framework and support necessary for the mission's success. This section examines the UN's involvement in planning, coordinating, and overseeing the peacekeeping operation, underscoring the significance of international cooperation under the UN umbrella.

Security Challenges and Strategies in Venezuela's Border Regions

Venezuela's border regions presented numerous security challenges that necessitated multinational cooperation. This subchapter analyzes the security threats faced by the region and explores the strategies employed by the multinational forces to address them effectively.

Humanitarian Aid Delivery in Operation Alba

Operation Alba not only focused on security but also had a strong humanitarian component. The subchapter discusses the importance of multinational cooperation in delivering essential aid to vulnerable populations, highlighting successful initiatives and assessing areas for improvement.

Multinational Cooperation and Coordination in Peacekeeping Efforts

The subchapter emphasizes the significance of effective coordination and cooperation among participating nations and organizations. It explores the mechanisms established to facilitate communication, decision-making, and the sharing of resources, emphasizing the benefits and challenges of such cooperation.

Impact of Operation Alba on Venezuelan Communities and Civilians

Operation Alba had a profound impact on Venezuelan communities and civilians, both positive and negative. This section examines the various social, economic, and political consequences of the peacekeeping mission, shedding light on the long-term effects on the affected populations.

Peace Negotiation and Diplomacy in Operation Alba

Peace negotiation and diplomacy played a crucial role in Operation Alba. This subchapter explores the diplomatic efforts undertaken by the multinational forces to promote dialogue and reconciliation, examining their effectiveness and lessons learned.

Role of Non-Governmental Organizations (NGOs) in Supporting Operation Alba

NGOs played a vital role in supporting Operation Alba, providing essential services and resources to complement the efforts of the multinational forces. This section discusses the contributions and challenges faced by NGOs in the peacekeeping mission.

Gender Perspectives in Peacekeeping Operations in Venezuela's Border Regions

This subchapter highlights the importance of gender perspectives in peacekeeping operations, specifically focusing on their relevance in the context of Operation Alba. It examines the efforts made to address gender-based violence, promote gender equality, and ensure the meaningful participation of women in peacebuilding processes.

Evaluating the Effectiveness of Operation Alba in Maintaining Peace and Stability

The subchapter evaluates the effectiveness of Operation Alba in achieving its objectives, assessing the impact of multinational cooperation on the mission's success. It examines the lessons learned and provides recommendations for future peacekeeping efforts.

Media Coverage and Public Opinion of Operation Alba in Venezuela and Internationally

The final section explores the role of media coverage and public opinion in shaping the perception of Operation Alba, both within Venezuela and internationally. It analyzes the media's portrayal of the peacekeeping mission and its impact on public perception and support.

In conclusion, the subchapter "Importance of Multinational Cooperation in Peacekeeping" delves into the significance of collaboration among different nations and organizations in peacekeeping efforts, with a specific focus on Operation Alba. It analyzes the various aspects of the mission, highlights its impact on Venezuelan communities and civilians, and evaluates its effectiveness in maintaining peace and stability. The subchapter also explores the role of media coverage and public opinion in shaping the perception of the peacekeeping mission.

Coordination Mechanisms in Operation Alba

In the realm of peacekeeping missions, effective coordination mechanisms are essential for the success of any multinational operation. Operation Alba, the 2020 multinational peacekeeping mission in Venezuela's border regions, demonstrated the significance of coordination in achieving peace and stability. This subchapter delves into the various coordination mechanisms employed in Operation Alba, shedding light on their effectiveness and contribution to the mission's overall objectives.

One of the key coordination mechanisms in Operation Alba was the role of the United Nations. As an international organization dedicated to maintaining peace and security, the UN played a pivotal role in overseeing and guiding the mission. Their expertise and experience in peacekeeping operations provided a solid foundation for effective coordination among the participating nations.

Another crucial coordination mechanism was the establishment of a joint command structure. Under this structure, representatives from each participating nation worked together to develop a comprehensive strategy and coordinate their efforts. This joint command structure ensured that all actions were harmonized and aligned with the mission's objectives, maximizing the impact of the peacekeeping operation.

Furthermore, Operation Alba emphasized the importance of coordination in delivering humanitarian aid. In conflict-affected regions, access to basic necessities becomes scarce, making humanitarian aid delivery a critical component of peacekeeping efforts. Through close coordination with non-governmental organizations (NGOs), Operation Alba was able to efficiently distribute aid to affected communities, providing them with much-needed support and alleviating their plight.

Gender perspectives also played a significant role in the coordination mechanisms of Operation Alba. Recognizing the unique challenges faced by women and girls in conflict zones, the mission incorporated a gender perspective into its operations. This involved coordination with local organizations and stakeholders to ensure the provision of gender-sensitive assistance and protection measures.

The effectiveness of these coordination mechanisms in Operation Alba can be evaluated by examining their impact on peace and stability in Venezuela's border regions. By maintaining open lines of communication, harmonizing strategies, and efficiently delivering aid, Operation Alba aimed to create a secure environment conducive to peace negotiations and diplomacy.

In conclusion, coordination mechanisms served as the backbone of Operation Alba, enabling multinational cooperation and facilitating the mission's various objectives. The role of the United Nations, joint command structures, collaboration with NGOs, and the integration of gender perspectives all contributed to the effectiveness of Operation Alba in maintaining peace and stability. By analyzing these coordination mechanisms, historians can gain valuable insights into the complexities of multinational peacekeeping efforts and their impact on both local communities and international relations.

Lessons Learned from Multinational Cooperation in Operation Alba

Operation Alba, the multinational peacekeeping mission carried out in Venezuela's border regions in 2020, provides valuable insights into the challenges, strategies, and impact of multinational cooperation in peacekeeping efforts. This subchapter explores the lessons learned from this mission, shedding light on various aspects that may be of interest to historians and the niches involved in Operation Alba.

One of the most significant lessons learned from Operation Alba is the crucial role played by the United Nations in facilitating and coordinating multinational cooperation. The UN's involvement ensured a unified approach, harmonized efforts, and promoted effective communication among participating nations. Historians studying peacekeeping operations can gain insights into the relevance of international organizations in such missions.

Furthermore, Operation Alba highlighted the security challenges faced in Venezuela's border regions and the strategies employed to address them. The subchapter delves into the complexities of maintaining peace and stability in a volatile environment, offering valuable lessons for those interested in security studies and conflict resolution. It explores the various strategies employed, such as intelligence sharing, joint patrols, and capacity building, and assesses their effectiveness in countering security threats.

The subchapter also examines the humanitarian aid delivery during Operation Alba. It analyzes the challenges faced by peacekeeping forces in providing assistance to affected communities and explores the strategies used to ensure effective humanitarian aid delivery. Historians interested in the intersection of humanitarian efforts and peacekeeping missions will find this analysis valuable.

Additionally, Operation Alba offers insights into the importance of multinational cooperation and coordination in peacekeeping efforts. The subchapter explores the mechanisms established to facilitate cooperation among participating nations, highlighting the significance of trust-building, information sharing, and joint decision-making. This analysis provides valuable lessons for policymakers and practitioners involved in peacekeeping operations.

The impact of Operation Alba on Venezuelan communities and civilians is another critical aspect addressed in this subchapter. It examines the positive outcomes, such as improved security, access to humanitarian aid, and enhanced socio-economic conditions, as well as the challenges faced in achieving lasting peace and stability. Historians interested in the long-term effects of peacekeeping missions on local populations will find this analysis insightful.

Moreover, the subchapter explores the role of non-governmental organizations (NGOs) in supporting Operation Alba. It examines the contributions made by NGOs in delivering humanitarian aid, facilitating dialogue, and advocating for the rights of vulnerable populations. This analysis sheds light on the importance of collaboration between state and non-state actors in peacekeeping operations.

Lastly, the subchapter evaluates the effectiveness of Operation Alba in maintaining peace and stability. It analyzes the mission's objectives, strategies, and outcomes, providing a comprehensive assessment of its overall impact. Historians interested in evaluating the success of peacekeeping missions will find this analysis useful.

Overall, this subchapter offers valuable lessons learned from multinational cooperation in Operation Alba. It provides insights into the role of the United Nations, security challenges and strategies, humanitarian aid delivery, coordination among participating nations, impact on local communities, NGO involvement, and the mission's overall effectiveness. Historians and the niches involved in Operation Alba will find this content informative and thought-provoking.

Chapter 6: Impact of Operation Alba on Venezuelan Communities and Civilians

Improved Security and Stability in Border Regions

The subchapter "Improved Security and Stability in Border Regions" delves into the significant strides made during Operation Alba, the 2020 multinational peacekeeping mission in Venezuela's border regions. This section highlights the efforts undertaken to enhance security and stability in these areas, shedding light on the various strategies, challenges, and the ultimate impact of this operation on Venezuelan communities and civilians.

Operation Alba recognized the dire need to address security challenges in Venezuela's border regions, which had been plagued by violence, organized crime, and instability. The mission aimed to restore peace and establish a safe environment for the local population, while also creating conditions for humanitarian aid delivery and promoting socio-economic development.

One of the key strategies employed during Operation Alba was multinational cooperation and coordination. By bringing together a diverse range of countries and their respective military forces, the mission was able to leverage a wealth of expertise and resources. This collaboration facilitated the sharing of best practices and the development of comprehensive security measures. Joint patrols, intelligence sharing, and coordinated border control operations significantly contributed to improved security in these vulnerable regions.

Furthermore, the role of the United Nations in Operation Alba cannot be overstated. The organization played a vital role in facilitating dialogue and negotiation between the participating nations, as well as providing critical logistical support and oversight. The UN's presence ensured adherence to international standards and protocols, bolstering the legitimacy and effectiveness of the mission.

The subchapter also explores the impact of Operation Alba on Venezuelan communities and civilians. Through enhanced security measures, the mission created a conducive environment for the delivery of humanitarian aid. This enabled the provision of much-needed medical assistance, food, and basic necessities to vulnerable populations. By addressing the security challenges, Operation Alba also laid the foundation for long-term development and stability in these border regions.

In conclusion, "Improved Security and Stability in Border Regions" highlights the successful strategies and collaboration employed during Operation Alba. The mission's efforts not only improved security but also paved the way for humanitarian aid delivery, socio-economic development, and long-term peace and stability in Venezuela's border regions. This subchapter sheds light on the transformative impact of the multinational peacekeeping mission and its significance in maintaining peace and security in the region.

Humanitarian Assistance and its Impact on Local Communities

Humanitarian assistance plays a crucial role in peacekeeping missions, and Operation Alba is no exception. This subchapter will explore the impact of humanitarian assistance on local communities in Venezuela's border regions, focusing on the lessons learned from Operation Alba.

One of the primary goals of Operation Alba was to provide much-needed humanitarian aid to the communities affected by the ongoing conflict in Venezuela. The multinational peacekeeping mission recognized the importance of addressing the immediate needs of the local population, including access to food, clean water, healthcare, and shelter. By delivering these essential services, Operation Alba aimed to alleviate the suffering and improve the overall well-being of the affected communities.

The impact of humanitarian assistance on local communities during Operation Alba was significant. The provision of aid not only met the basic needs of the population but also helped restore a sense of normalcy and stability. By addressing the root causes of conflict and providing essential services, Operation Alba contributed to the resilience and recovery of the affected communities.

Furthermore, the effectiveness of humanitarian assistance in Operation Alba was enhanced through the coordination and cooperation among multinational actors, non-governmental organizations (NGOs), and the United Nations. These partnerships allowed for the efficient and timely delivery of aid, ensuring that it reached the most vulnerable populations.

The impact of humanitarian assistance was not limited to the immediate relief provided. It also had wider implications for the peace and stability of the region. By addressing the needs of the local population, Operation Alba created an environment conducive to peace negotiations and diplomacy. The provision of aid helped build trust and fostered a sense of goodwill among the communities, facilitating dialogue and reconciliation.

However, it is essential to evaluate the effectiveness of Operation Alba in maintaining peace and stability in the region. The subchapter will analyze the outcomes and consequences of the mission, considering both the positive and negative aspects. Furthermore, it will explore the role of media coverage and public opinion in shaping international perceptions of Operation Alba and its impact on Venezuelan communities.

In conclusion, humanitarian assistance played a vital role in Operation Alba, positively impacting local communities in Venezuela's border regions. By addressing the immediate needs of the population and fostering an environment conducive to peace and stability, Operation Alba contributed to the overall well-being and resilience of the affected communities. However, further evaluation is required to determine the long-term effectiveness of the mission and the role of various stakeholders, including NGOs, in supporting the peacekeeping efforts in Venezuela.

Challenges Faced by Venezuelan Communities during Operation Alba

Introduction:

Operation Alba, the 2020 multinational peacekeeping mission in Venezuela's border regions, aimed to restore peace and stability in a region plagued by violence and insecurity. However, the mission was not without its challenges. This subchapter explores the various difficulties faced by Venezuelan communities during Operation Alba and the impact it had on their lives.

1. Security Challenges:

Venezuela's border regions have long been plagued by armed groups, drug trafficking, and organized crime. Operation Alba faced significant security challenges in dealing with these non-state actors, who often targeted civilian populations. The presence of peacekeepers did not eliminate the threat entirely, leading to fear and anxiety among local communities.

2. Humanitarian Aid Delivery:

The delivery of humanitarian aid was a crucial aspect of Operation Alba. However, logistical challenges and bureaucratic hurdles posed significant obstacles. The lack of infrastructure and resources, coupled with corruption, made it difficult to reach vulnerable communities in need.

As a result, many Venezuelans continued to suffer from food and medical shortages.

3. Coordination and Cooperation:

Multinational cooperation was vital for the success of Operation Alba. However, coordinating efforts between different countries, the United Nations, and non-governmental organizations (NGOs) was not without its difficulties. Language barriers, differing priorities, and conflicting strategies often hindered effective collaboration, impacting the overall mission's effectiveness.

4. Gender Perspectives:

Gender perspectives in peacekeeping operations are crucial to ensuring the protection and empowerment of women in conflict-affected areas. However, during Operation Alba, gender-specific challenges surfaced. Women and girls faced increased vulnerability to sexual violence, exploitation, and trafficking. Addressing these issues required greater focus and resources.

5. Impact on Venezuelan Communities:

Operation Alba had a significant impact on Venezuelan communities and civilians. While it aimed to bring peace and stability, the presence of peacekeepers sometimes caused fear and mistrust among the local population. Moreover, the mission's limited resources often meant that not all communities could be adequately supported, leading to feelings of inequality and resentment.

Conclusion:

Operation Alba faced numerous challenges in its mission to restore peace and stability in Venezuela's border regions. From security threats to logistical hurdles, these difficulties had a direct impact on the lives of

Venezuelan communities. Recognizing and addressing these challenges is crucial for future peacekeeping efforts to effectively support and protect vulnerable populations in conflict-affected regions.

Chapter 7: Peace Negotiation and Diplomacy in Operation Alba

Role of Negotiation and Diplomacy in Peacekeeping Operations

The Role of Negotiation and Diplomacy in Peacekeeping Operations

In the realm of peacekeeping operations, negotiation and diplomacy play a crucial role in achieving and maintaining peace and stability. This subchapter titled "Role of Negotiation and Diplomacy in Peacekeeping Operations" delves into the significance of these tools in the context of Operation Alba, the multinational peacekeeping mission in Venezuela's border regions in 2020.

Operation Alba: The 2020 Multinational Peacekeeping Mission in Venezuela's Border Regions

Operation Alba, a pivotal peacekeeping mission in Venezuela's border regions, witnessed the extensive use of negotiation and diplomacy to address the complex security challenges and humanitarian crisis in the area. This subchapter sheds light on how negotiation and diplomacy were employed to foster cooperation and coordination among participating nations.

Role of the United Nations in Operation Alba

The United Nations played a central role in facilitating negotiation and diplomacy throughout Operation Alba. By leveraging its diplomatic channels, the UN was able to bring together various stakeholders and foster dialogue to resolve conflicts and promote peace in the region. This subchapter explores the specific strategies employed by the UN in supporting negotiation and diplomacy in Operation Alba.

Peace Negotiation and Diplomacy in Operation Alba

Negotiation and diplomacy played a pivotal role in peace negotiations during Operation Alba. This subchapter delves into the specific instances where negotiation and diplomacy were employed to broker peace agreements and facilitate dialogue between conflicting parties. It also explores the challenges encountered during these negotiations and the lessons learned from the process.

Role of Non-Governmental Organizations (NGOs) in Supporting Operation Alba

Non-governmental organizations (NGOs) played a crucial role in supporting Operation Alba by employing negotiation and diplomacy to provide humanitarian aid and support to affected communities. This subchapter examines the contributions of NGOs in the peacekeeping efforts and how their use of negotiation and diplomacy helped bridge gaps and address the needs of vulnerable populations.

Evaluating the Effectiveness of Operation Alba in Maintaining Peace and Stability

This subchapter critically evaluates the effectiveness of negotiation and diplomacy in Operation Alba in maintaining peace and stability in Venezuela's border regions. It analyzes the successes and shortcomings of the mission and provides insights on how negotiation and diplomacy can be further optimized in future peacekeeping operations.

Overall, the role of negotiation and diplomacy in peacekeeping operations, as exemplified in Operation Alba, is essential in resolving conflicts, fostering cooperation, and bringing about sustainable peace. This subchapter aims to provide historians and the niches of Operation Alba with a comprehensive understanding of the significance of negotiation and diplomacy in peacekeeping efforts.

Diplomatic Efforts in Operation Alba

Diplomatic efforts played a crucial role in the success of Operation Alba, the 2020 multinational peacekeeping mission in Venezuela's border regions. This subchapter explores the various diplomatic strategies and negotiations that took place during the mission, shedding light on their significance and impact.

One of the key diplomatic endeavors in Operation Alba was the role of the United Nations. As an international organization dedicated to maintaining peace and security, the UN played a vital part in facilitating dialogue and negotiations between the involved parties. Through its diplomatic channels, the UN helped to establish a framework for cooperation and coordination among the multinational forces, the Venezuelan government, and other stakeholders.

Furthermore, diplomatic efforts also focused on addressing the security challenges in Venezuela's border regions. Diplomats engaged in delicate negotiations with local authorities and armed groups to ensure a safe operating environment for the peacekeeping mission. These discussions often involved finding common ground, establishing trust, and developing strategies to tackle security threats effectively.

Another vital aspect of Operation Alba's diplomatic efforts was the delivery of humanitarian aid. Diplomats worked closely with non-governmental organizations (NGOs) to coordinate the provision of critical assistance to the affected communities. Through diplomatic channels, aid convoys were able to navigate logistical challenges and gain access to areas in need.

Peace negotiation and diplomacy were central to Operation Alba's objectives. Diplomats engaged in dialogue with various parties, including the Venezuelan government, armed groups, and community leaders, to promote understanding, trust, and reconciliation. These negotiations aimed to address the root causes of conflict and build a sustainable peace in the region.

Moreover, gender perspectives were integrated into the peacekeeping operations in Venezuela's border regions. Diplomatic efforts focused on promoting the inclusion and participation of women in decision-making processes, as well as addressing the specific needs and vulnerabilities of women and girls affected by the conflict.

The effectiveness of diplomatic efforts in Operation Alba can be evaluated through several lenses. Historians can analyze the outcomes of negotiations, the level of cooperation achieved, and the lasting impact on Venezuelan communities and civilians. Additionally, media coverage and public opinion of Operation Alba, both in Venezuela and internationally, can provide insights into the perception and effectiveness of diplomatic efforts.

In conclusion, diplomatic efforts played a vital role in Operation Alba, facilitating cooperation, negotiation, and humanitarian aid delivery. The United Nations, NGOs, and various stakeholders collaborated to address security challenges, promote peace negotiations, and ensure the well-being of affected communities. The effectiveness of these diplomatic efforts can be evaluated through multiple perspectives, shedding light on the lessons learned for future peacekeeping missions.

Achievements and Challenges in Peace Negotiation

In the subchapter "Achievements and Challenges in Peace Negotiation," we delve into the critical aspects of Operation Alba, a multinational peacekeeping mission in Venezuela's border regions. This section aims to provide historians and individuals interested in Operation Alba with a comprehensive understanding of the accomplishments and obstacles encountered during the peace negotiation process.

One of the significant achievements of Operation Alba was the successful establishment of a dialogue between conflicting parties. The peace negotiation efforts facilitated open communication and provided a platform for all parties involved to voice their concerns, grievances, and aspirations. This inclusive and participatory approach allowed for the exploration of potential common ground and the development of mutually agreeable solutions.

Another noteworthy achievement was the commitment to upholding the United Nations' role in Operation Alba. The involvement of the UN brought credibility, expertise, and resources to the peacekeeping mission. The organization played a crucial role in mediating negotiations, ensuring compliance with international laws and standards, and coordinating humanitarian aid delivery.

However, the peace negotiation process encountered several challenges. One of the primary obstacles was the complex security landscape in Venezuela's border regions. The presence of armed groups, criminal organizations, and political tensions posed significant threats to the peacekeeping efforts. Overcoming these challenges required innovative security strategies, intelligence sharing, and coordinated efforts among the participating nations.

Humanitarian aid delivery also presented challenges in Operation Alba. The volatile security situation, logistical constraints, and political constraints often hindered the timely and efficient delivery of aid to the affected communities. NGOs played a vital role in supporting Operation Alba by providing assistance on the ground, ensuring the effective distribution of aid, and addressing the specific needs of vulnerable groups, such as women and children.

Gender perspectives in peacekeeping operations emerged as another focal point during the peace negotiation process. Recognizing the unique experiences and contributions of women in conflict resolution and peacebuilding became an integral aspect of Operation Alba. Efforts were made to ensure the inclusion of women in decision-making processes and to address gender-based violence and discrimination.

Evaluating the effectiveness of Operation Alba in maintaining peace and stability is crucial. The subchapter will explore key indicators, such as the reduction of violence, the restoration of basic services, and the reintegration of ex-combatants into society. Additionally, media coverage and public opinion of Operation Alba, both within Venezuela and internationally, will be examined to understand the mission's perception and impact on the wider community.

In conclusion, the subchapter "Achievements and Challenges in Peace Negotiation" provides a comprehensive analysis of the successes and obstacles encountered in Operation Alba. It highlights the importance of inclusive dialogue, the role of the United Nations, security challenges, humanitarian aid delivery, gender perspectives, and the evaluation of peacekeeping effectiveness. This content aims to deepen the understanding of historians and individuals interested in the complexities of peace negotiation and the potential for multinational cooperation in maintaining peace and stability in conflict-affected regions.

Chapter 8: Role of Non-Governmental Organizations (NGOs) in Supporting Operation Alba

Importance of NGO Involvement in Peacekeeping Missions

The Importance of NGO Involvement in Peacekeeping Missions

In the realm of peacekeeping missions, the involvement of non-governmental organizations (NGOs) plays a pivotal role in ensuring the success and effectiveness of these operations. This subchapter aims to shed light on the significance of NGO involvement specifically in Operation Alba, the 2020 multinational peacekeeping mission in Venezuela's border regions. Addressed to historians and the niches interested in Operation Alba, this content will delve into the various ways in which NGOs contributed to this mission and its impact on Venezuelan communities and civilians.

First and foremost, NGOs bring a unique set of skills, expertise, and resources to peacekeeping missions. In Operation Alba, NGOs played a crucial role in providing humanitarian aid and delivering vital services to the affected communities. Their presence ensured the provision of essential supplies, medical assistance, and support to those most in need, particularly in the border regions. Their involvement helped alleviate the dire humanitarian situation and fostered a sense of security and stability within these communities.

Moreover, NGOs also acted as intermediaries between the peacekeeping forces and the local population. They played a vital role in building trust and establishing effective communication channels, which are essential for successful peace negotiations and diplomacy. NGOs, with their grassroots connections and local knowledge, were able to facilitate dialogue and bridge the gap between the peacekeeping forces, the government, and the affected communities.

Furthermore, NGOs bring a gender perspective to peacekeeping operations. In Venezuela's border regions, where women and girls are often disproportionately affected by conflict and insecurity, NGOs played a crucial role in addressing the specific needs and vulnerabilities of women and promoting gender equality. Their involvement ensured that women's voices were heard, and their rights were protected throughout the mission.

The impact of NGO involvement in Operation Alba cannot be overstated. Their presence not only provided immediate relief and support to the affected communities but also contributed to the long-term stability and peacebuilding efforts. By addressing the root causes of conflict and engaging in capacity-building initiatives, NGOs helped create a sustainable foundation for peace and development in Venezuela's border regions.

In conclusion, NGOs play a vital role in peacekeeping missions, as demonstrated by their involvement in Operation Alba. Their expertise, resources, and dedication to humanitarian causes make them indispensable partners in maintaining peace and stability. Their presence in the mission not only provided essential aid and services but also fostered trust, facilitated dialogue, and promoted gender equality. The impact of NGO involvement in Operation Alba extends far beyond the mission itself, creating a lasting positive effect on Venezuelan communities and civilians.

Contributions of NGOs in Operation Alba

Non-governmental organizations (NGOs) played a crucial role in supporting and enhancing the effectiveness of Operation Alba, the multinational peacekeeping mission in Venezuela's border regions in

2020. Their contributions spanned a wide range of areas, including humanitarian aid delivery, peace negotiation and diplomacy, and gender perspectives in peacekeeping operations.

One of the key contributions of NGOs was in the delivery of humanitarian aid to the vulnerable communities affected by the conflict in Venezuela's border regions. NGOs, with their expertise and network, were able to mobilize resources and provide essential supplies such as food, medical assistance, and shelter to the affected population. Their presence not only addressed the immediate needs of the communities but also helped build trust and establish rapport between the peacekeepers and the local people.

NGOs also played a significant role in peace negotiation and diplomacy during Operation Alba. Their impartiality and expertise in conflict resolution made them valuable intermediaries between the conflicting parties. NGOs facilitated dialogue, negotiated ceasefires, and supported the implementation of peace agreements. Their involvement helped build consensus and fostered an environment conducive to lasting peace and stability in the region.

Furthermore, NGOs brought a gender perspective to the peacekeeping operations in Venezuela's border regions. They advocated for the inclusion of women in decision-making processes and promoted gender equality in all aspects of the mission. NGOs worked to ensure that women's voices were heard, their rights protected, and their unique needs addressed. This gender-sensitive approach not only contributed to the overall effectiveness of Operation Alba but also laid the foundation for long-term peacebuilding efforts.

The contributions of NGOs in Operation Alba were instrumental in enhancing the effectiveness of the mission. Their involvement in humanitarian aid delivery, peace negotiation, and gender perspectives brought valuable expertise and resources to the table. By working in collaboration with the United Nations and other stakeholders, NGOs played a crucial role in maintaining peace and stability in Venezuela's border regions.

Through their efforts, NGOs not only provided immediate relief to the affected communities but also contributed to the long-term development and sustainability of peace in the region. Their contributions should be acknowledged and further supported to ensure the success of future peacekeeping missions.

Collaboration between NGOs and Operation Alba

The collaboration between non-governmental organizations (NGOs) and Operation Alba played a pivotal role in the success of the 2020 multinational peacekeeping mission in Venezuela's border regions. This subchapter aims to shed light on the significant contribution of NGOs in supporting and enhancing the effectiveness of Operation Alba.

NGOs, with their expertise and experience in humanitarian aid delivery, played a crucial role in providing much-needed support to the mission. These organizations were able to leverage their existing networks and resources to mobilize and coordinate humanitarian assistance, ensuring that it reached the affected communities in a timely and efficient manner. Their involvement helped bridge the gap between the peacekeeping forces and the local population, fostering trust and cooperation between the two.

One of the key areas where NGOs made a significant impact was in the delivery of humanitarian aid. Operation Alba faced numerous challenges in accessing remote and conflict-affected areas, but NGOs, with their local knowledge and connections, were able to navigate these obstacles effectively. They provided essential supplies, such as food, water, medical supplies, and shelter, to the affected communities, alleviating their suffering and contributing to the overall stability of the region.

Moreover, NGOs also played a vital role in addressing the specific needs of vulnerable groups, including women and children, in the peacekeeping operation. They ensured that gender perspectives were integrated into the mission's activities, advocating for the protection of women's rights, promoting gender equality, and providing support to survivors of gender-based violence. By doing so, NGOs helped create a more inclusive and equitable peacekeeping environment.

The collaboration between NGOs and Operation Alba extended beyond the delivery of humanitarian aid. These organizations also provided valuable expertise and insight on peace negotiation and diplomacy, drawing on their experience in conflict resolution and mediation. They facilitated dialogue between the conflicting parties, promoting peaceful resolutions and contributing to the overall success of the mission.

In evaluating the effectiveness of Operation Alba, the role of NGOs cannot be overlooked. Their collaboration and coordination with the peacekeeping forces played a crucial role in maintaining peace and stability in Venezuela's border regions. Furthermore, their efforts garnered significant media coverage and public opinion, both domestically and internationally, shedding light on the importance of multinational cooperation in peacekeeping operations.

Overall, the collaboration between NGOs and Operation Alba served as a model for effective and efficient peacekeeping efforts. Their joint efforts in delivering humanitarian aid, promoting gender perspectives, facilitating peace negotiations, and raising public awareness contributed to the overall success of the mission and had a positive impact on Venezuelan communities and civilians.

Chapter 9: Gender Perspectives in Peacekeeping Operations in Venezuela's Border Regions

Importance of Gender Mainstreaming in Peacekeeping

Gender mainstreaming is a crucial aspect of peacekeeping operations, and its significance cannot be overstated. In the context of Operation Alba, the multinational peacekeeping mission in Venezuela's border regions, the incorporation of gender perspectives and the promotion of gender equality are of utmost importance in ensuring the effectiveness and sustainability of the mission. This subchapter delves into the importance of gender mainstreaming in peacekeeping, shedding light on its various dimensions and implications.

One of the primary reasons why gender mainstreaming is essential in peacekeeping is its potential to enhance the comprehensiveness and appropriateness of peacekeeping strategies and interventions. By considering the different experiences, needs, and perspectives of men, women, girls, and boys, peacekeeping forces can devise more targeted and effective approaches to address the root causes of conflict and promote lasting peace. Gender mainstreaming ensures that peacekeeping efforts are not one-size-fits-all but rather tailored to the specific needs and vulnerabilities of different groups within the society.

Furthermore, gender mainstreaming contributes to the protection and promotion of human rights, particularly those of women and girls, who are often disproportionately affected by conflict. Women and girls face unique challenges during conflict situations, including sexual and gender-based violence, displacement, and limited access to resources and services. By prioritizing gender mainstreaming in peacekeeping, Operation Alba can actively work towards addressing these issues and ensuring the safety, well-being, and empowerment of women and girls in the border regions of Venezuela.

In addition to these practical considerations, gender mainstreaming also has normative and ethical implications. It aligns with the principles of equality, non-discrimination, and human rights, which form the foundation of peacekeeping operations. By integrating gender perspectives into all aspects of peacekeeping, including decision-making, policy formulation, planning, and implementation, Operation Alba can uphold these principles and contribute to a more just and inclusive society.

Moreover, gender mainstreaming in peacekeeping can serve as a catalyst for societal transformation. By challenging traditional gender norms and stereotypes, peacekeeping forces can contribute to the empowerment of women and the promotion of gender equality in the long run. This, in turn, can foster social cohesion, reduce inequalities, and build a more resilient and peaceful society in the border regions of Venezuela.

To fully realize the potential of gender mainstreaming in peacekeeping, concerted efforts are required at all levels. Operation Alba should invest in gender training and capacity-building for its personnel, ensuring that they have the necessary knowledge and skills to integrate gender perspectives into their work. Collaboration with local communities, civil society organizations, and non-governmental organizations (NGOs) that specialize in gender issues is also crucial. By working together, these stakeholders can create a comprehensive and sustainable approach to gender mainstreaming in peacekeeping, thereby maximizing the positive impact of Operation Alba on Venezuelan communities and civilians.

In conclusion, gender mainstreaming is of utmost importance in peacekeeping, including in the context of Operation Alba. By incorporating gender perspectives and promoting gender equality, peacekeeping forces can enhance the effectiveness, comprehensiveness, and sustainability of their interventions. Moreover, gender mainstreaming aligns with principles of equality, human rights, and societal transformation, making it an ethical imperative. By prioritizing gender mainstreaming, Operation Alba can contribute to a more just, inclusive, and peaceful society in the border regions of Venezuela.

Gender Perspectives in Operation Alba

In the context of Operation Alba, a multinational peacekeeping mission in Venezuela's border regions, it is imperative to analyze and understand the gender perspectives that influenced the success and impact of the mission. Gender perspectives in peacekeeping operations play a crucial role in ensuring inclusivity, effectiveness, and long-term stability.

Operation Alba, initiated in 2020, aimed to address the security challenges in Venezuela's border regions and provide humanitarian aid to the affected communities. However, it is essential to note that conflict and crises affect men, women, and children differently. Therefore, a gender-sensitive approach is essential in understanding the complex dynamics on the ground.

Firstly, gender perspectives in Operation Alba help identify the specific security challenges faced by women and girls in the border regions. Women often face unique risks such as sexual and gender-based violence, trafficking, and exploitation. By understanding these challenges, the peacekeeping mission can develop strategies that protect and empower women and girls, ensuring their safety and well-being.

Secondly, gender perspectives also shed light on the role of women in peace negotiations and diplomacy. Women have historically been underrepresented in peace processes, despite their vital contributions to conflict resolution and peacebuilding. Operation Alba must actively involve women in decision-making processes to ensure a more inclusive and sustainable peace agreement.

Moreover, gender perspectives are crucial in evaluating the effectiveness of Operation Alba in maintaining peace and stability. By analyzing the impact of the mission on different genders, historians can assess whether the mission has addressed the specific needs and priorities of women, men, and marginalized groups. This evaluation will help identify areas for improvement and ensure that future peacekeeping efforts are more inclusive and successful.

Furthermore, the role of non-governmental organizations (NGOs) in supporting Operation Alba cannot be overlooked. NGOs often play a significant role in providing gender-responsive humanitarian aid, addressing the specific needs of women and girls. Historians need to examine the collaboration between peacekeeping forces and NGOs to understand how gender perspectives were integrated into the delivery of humanitarian aid.

In conclusion, gender perspectives in Operation Alba are essential for a comprehensive understanding of the mission's impact on Venezuelan communities. By analyzing the specific challenges faced by women and girls, involving women in peace negotiations, and evaluating the mission's effectiveness through a gender lens, historians can contribute to the development of more inclusive and effective peacekeeping efforts in the future. This subchapter serves as a critical resource for historians and scholars interested in the gender dynamics of Operation Alba and its implications for peacekeeping operations globally.

Challenges and Progress in Ensuring Gender Equality

In the realm of peacekeeping operations, ensuring gender equality has emerged as a critical challenge that requires continuous attention and effort. Operation Alba, the multinational peacekeeping mission in Venezuela's border regions, is no exception to this, as it faces its own set of obstacles and achievements in promoting gender equality. This subchapter examines the challenges encountered and the progress made in this crucial area.

One of the initial challenges faced by Operation Alba was the underrepresentation of women in peacekeeping forces. Historically, peacekeeping missions have been male-dominated, which hampers the ability to fully address the needs and concerns of women and girls in conflict-affected communities. However, Operation Alba has made significant progress in this regard by actively recruiting and deploying more women peacekeepers. This deliberate effort has not only increased the gender balance within the mission but has also fostered a more inclusive and gender-sensitive approach to peacekeeping.

Another challenge that Operation Alba has encountered is the persistence of gender-based violence in the border regions of Venezuela. Conflict and instability exacerbate existing inequalities, leaving women and girls particularly vulnerable to various forms of violence, including sexual exploitation and abuse. Operation Alba has responded to this challenge by implementing robust measures to prevent and respond to gender-based violence. These measures include training peacekeepers on gender equality, establishing safe spaces for women and girls, and collaborating with local organizations to provide support and services to survivors.

Furthermore, Operation Alba has recognized the importance of women's participation in peace negotiations and decision-making processes. Women's perspectives and experiences are crucial in shaping policies and strategies that promote sustainable peace and stability. The mission has actively engaged with local women's organizations and leaders, providing them with a platform to voice their concerns and contribute to peacebuilding efforts.

While Operation Alba has made commendable progress in promoting gender equality, there are still areas that require further attention.

Despite efforts to address gender-based violence, more resources and support are needed to ensure adequate protection and assistance for survivors. Additionally, the mission should continue to prioritize the inclusion of women in leadership positions and decision-making roles.

In conclusion, Operation Alba faces both challenges and progress in ensuring gender equality in Venezuela's border regions. By actively recruiting women peacekeepers, addressing gender-based violence, and promoting women's participation in peace processes, the mission has taken significant steps towards achieving gender parity. However, ongoing efforts are required to overcome remaining obstacles and fully integrate a gender perspective into peacekeeping operations. By doing so, Operation Alba can contribute to a more inclusive and sustainable peace in Venezuela.

Chapter 10: Evaluating the Effectiveness of Operation Alba in Maintaining Peace and Stability

Criteria for Evaluating Peacekeeping Missions

Evaluating peacekeeping missions is crucial to understanding their effectiveness in maintaining peace and stability in conflict-affected regions. This subchapter explores the criteria for evaluating peacekeeping missions, with a specific focus on Operation Alba, the 2020 multinational peacekeeping mission in Venezuela's border regions. Historians and those interested in Operation Alba will find this analysis valuable in assessing the mission's impact on Venezuelan communities and civilians.

One essential criterion for evaluating peacekeeping missions is the ability to maintain the ceasefire and prevent the resurgence of violence. In the case of Operation Alba, historians can assess whether the mission effectively prevented armed conflicts from erupting in the border regions of Venezuela. This criterion also encompasses the mission's success in disarming and demobilizing armed groups, thus contributing to long-term stability.

Another crucial aspect is the delivery of humanitarian aid to the affected populations. Evaluating Operation Alba's performance in this regard involves examining the effectiveness of aid distribution, ensuring that it reaches the most vulnerable individuals and communities. Historians can analyze the mission's ability to coordinate with local actors and non-governmental organizations (NGOs) to provide timely and adequate assistance.

Furthermore, evaluating multinational cooperation and coordination is essential to understanding the mission's overall effectiveness. Operation

Alba involved multiple nations and organizations, making coordination a complex task. Historians can examine the level of cooperation between participating countries, the United Nations, and NGOs to evaluate the mission's ability to work together towards shared goals.

Gender perspectives in peacekeeping operations are increasingly recognized as crucial for successful missions. Historians can evaluate Operation Alba's approach to integrating gender perspectives, such as ensuring the participation and protection of women in peace processes and addressing gender-based violence in the conflict-affected regions.

Lastly, media coverage and public opinion play a significant role in shaping the perception of peacekeeping missions. Historians can analyze the media coverage and public opinion of Operation Alba in Venezuela and internationally to gauge the mission's legitimacy and public support.

By considering these criteria, historians can comprehensively evaluate the effectiveness of Operation Alba in maintaining peace and stability in Venezuela's border regions. This evaluation will provide valuable insights into the mission's impact on Venezuelan communities and civilians, the role of the United Nations, NGOs, and non-state actors, as well as the challenges faced in achieving the mission's objectives. Ultimately, this analysis will contribute to a deeper understanding of multinational cooperation in peacekeeping efforts and inform future peacekeeping missions.

Successes and Failures of Operation Alba

Operation Alba was a multinational peacekeeping mission launched in 2020 in Venezuela's border regions. This subchapter focuses on the successes and failures of this operation, providing a comprehensive analysis of its impact and effectiveness.

One of the key successes of Operation Alba was the successful delivery of humanitarian aid to the affected communities in Venezuela's border regions. Despite the challenging security situation, the mission was able to provide much-needed assistance to the vulnerable population, including food, medical supplies, and shelter. This helped alleviate the suffering of the local communities and demonstrated the commitment of the international community to their well-being.

Another success of Operation Alba was the effective coordination and cooperation among the participating nations. The mission involved multiple countries, each with their own military and logistical capabilities. However, through joint planning and cooperation, the mission was able to overcome these challenges and work together towards a common goal. This demonstrated the importance of multinational cooperation in peacekeeping efforts.

However, Operation Alba also faced several failures and challenges. One of the major failures was the inability to fully address the security challenges in Venezuela's border regions. Despite the presence of peacekeeping forces, armed groups and criminal organizations continued to operate, posing a threat to the stability and safety of the local population. This highlighted the complexity of the security situation and the need for a more comprehensive approach to address these challenges.

Additionally, the peace negotiation and diplomacy efforts in Operation Alba were not entirely successful. While some progress was made in initiating dialogue between conflicting parties, a lasting peace agreement was not reached. This failure highlighted the underlying political and social complexities in Venezuela and the difficulties in achieving sustainable peace through military intervention alone.

Another challenge faced by Operation Alba was the limited involvement of non-governmental organizations (NGOs) in supporting the mission. Despite their expertise and experience in humanitarian assistance, their participation was not fully utilized. This limited the effectiveness of the mission in providing comprehensive support to the affected communities.

In conclusion, Operation Alba had both successes and failures. While it achieved significant milestones in delivering humanitarian aid and promoting multinational cooperation, it also faced challenges in addressing security concerns and achieving a lasting peace agreement. The lessons learned from this mission can provide valuable insights for future peacekeeping efforts in Venezuela and beyond.

Lessons Learned for Future Peacekeeping Efforts

As historians delve into the complexities of Operation Alba, the 2020 multinational peacekeeping mission in Venezuela's border regions, it becomes imperative to draw valuable lessons for future peacekeeping efforts. This subchapter aims to shed light on the key insights gained from Operation Alba, which may prove instrumental in shaping more effective and impactful peacekeeping missions in the future.

One crucial lesson that emerges from Operation Alba is the paramount role of multinational cooperation and coordination in peacekeeping efforts. The success of this mission was largely predicated on the ability of diverse nations to come together, pooling their resources, expertise, and military capabilities, to address the security challenges prevalent in Venezuela's border regions. It is evident that future peacekeeping missions should prioritize and foster international collaboration to ensure a comprehensive and unified approach.

Additionally, the role of the United Nations in Operation Alba serves as another valuable lesson. The UN's involvement, through its specialized agencies and peacekeeping forces, played a pivotal role in facilitating humanitarian aid delivery and promoting peace negotiations and diplomacy. This underscores the significance of the UN's mediation and facilitation in achieving peaceful resolutions and maintaining stability in conflict-ridden regions.

Operation Alba also shed light on the importance of engaging non-governmental organizations (NGOs) in supporting peacekeeping efforts. NGOs played a critical role in providing humanitarian aid and assistance to affected communities and civilians. Their involvement showcased the necessity of leveraging their expertise and resources to effectively address the multifaceted challenges faced during peacekeeping missions.

Moreover, gender perspectives in peacekeeping operations emerged as a key area for consideration. Operation Alba highlighted the importance of integrating gender-sensitive approaches in peacekeeping efforts, ensuring the protection and empowerment of women and marginalized groups. Future peacekeeping missions must prioritize gender equality and inclusivity to foster sustainable peace and stability.

Lastly, evaluating the effectiveness of Operation Alba in maintaining peace and stability provides valuable insights into refining future peacekeeping strategies. Understanding the impact of this mission on Venezuelan communities and civilians, as well as analyzing media coverage and public opinion, can guide policymakers and stakeholders in making informed decisions and improving the efficacy of future peacekeeping endeavors.

In conclusion, Operation Alba offers a wealth of lessons for future peacekeeping efforts. The importance of multinational cooperation, the role of the United Nations, the involvement of NGOs, gender perspectives, and thorough evaluation are all critical components to consider. By heeding these lessons, historians and policymakers can contribute to the development of more effective and impactful peacekeeping missions in the years to come.

Chapter 11: Media Coverage and Public Opinion of Operation Alba in Venezuela and Internationally

Role of Media in Shaping Public Perception

The Role of Media in Shaping Public Perception

In the modern age, media plays a significant role in shaping public perception, and this is particularly evident in the context of peacekeeping missions such as Operation Alba in Venezuela's border regions. The media acts as a powerful tool for disseminating information and influencing public opinion, making it crucial to understand its impact on shaping people's perception of the mission.

Operation Alba, a multinational peacekeeping mission conducted in 2020, faced numerous challenges and complexities in Venezuela's border regions. However, the success or failure of the mission was not solely determined by the actions on the ground but also by how it was portrayed by the media. The media has the power to highlight certain aspects of the mission while downplaying others, ultimately shaping public perception.

For historians studying Operation Alba, analyzing media coverage becomes essential in understanding the impact of the mission on Venezuelan communities and civilians. Media coverage can shed light on the effectiveness of the mission in maintaining peace and stability, as well as the challenges faced by the peacekeepers. It can also provide insights into the role of the United Nations and non-governmental organizations (NGOs) in supporting the mission.

Furthermore, media coverage can offer gender perspectives in peacekeeping operations in Venezuela's border regions. By examining the portrayal of women's roles in the mission, historians can evaluate the extent to which gender equality and women's empowerment were integrated into the peacekeeping efforts.

Moreover, media coverage is not limited to the domestic audience but also influences international perceptions of Operation Alba. Historians need to examine how the media portrayed the mission on the global stage and how this influenced international support and involvement. Media coverage can also shed light on the role of non-governmental organizations (NGOs) in supporting Operation Alba and their impact on public perception.

Understanding the role of media in shaping public perception is crucial for evaluating the effectiveness of Operation Alba and its impact on Venezuelan communities. By analyzing media coverage, historians can gain valuable insights into the challenges, strategies, and outcomes of the mission. This subchapter aims to delve into the depth of media coverage and its influence on public opinion, providing a comprehensive understanding of the role of media in shaping public perception of Operation Alba in Venezuela and internationally.

Media Coverage of Operation Alba in Venezuela

The media plays a crucial role in shaping public opinion and perception of peacekeeping missions such as Operation Alba. In the case of Operation Alba, the media coverage has been both influential and controversial, as it has had an impact on how the mission is perceived both in Venezuela and internationally.

Since its inception in 2020, Operation Alba has been closely followed by journalists and news outlets from around the world. The mission's objective to restore peace and stability in Venezuela's border regions has garnered significant attention due to the ongoing political and humanitarian crisis in the country. Media coverage has provided a platform for the voices of those affected by the conflict, shedding light on the suffering and struggles of Venezuelan communities and civilians.

However, media coverage of Operation Alba has not been without its challenges. The polarized political landscape in Venezuela has led to biased reporting, with different news outlets portraying the mission in accordance with their own agendas. This has resulted in conflicting narratives and a lack of consensus on the effectiveness of the mission.

International media outlets have also played a significant role in shaping public opinion of Operation Alba. Their coverage has highlighted the involvement of multinational actors, such as the United Nations, in the peacekeeping efforts. This has helped to generate support and awareness for the mission on a global scale.

The role of social media in shaping public opinion of Operation Alba cannot be understated. Platforms such as Twitter and Facebook have allowed for real-time updates and citizen journalism, providing a platform for voices that may otherwise go unheard. However, the spread of misinformation and fake news on social media has also posed challenges, as it can distort public perception and undermine the mission's objectives.

In conclusion, media coverage of Operation Alba in Venezuela has played a significant role in shaping public opinion and perception of the mission. While it has provided a platform for the voices of those affected by the conflict, it has also faced challenges such as biased reporting and the spread of misinformation. As historians, it is crucial to critically analyze media coverage to gain a comprehensive understanding of the impact of Operation Alba on Venezuelan communities and its effectiveness in maintaining peace and stability.

International Perception and Reaction to Operation Alba

Operation Alba, the multinational peacekeeping mission in Venezuela's border regions, garnered significant attention and evoked varied perceptions and reactions from the international community. Historians and those interested in Operation Alba will find this subchapter crucial in understanding the global response to this unprecedented endeavor.

From its inception, Operation Alba faced scrutiny and skepticism from some nations. Critics questioned the legality and legitimacy of the intervention, emphasizing the importance of respecting national sovereignty. These concerns were particularly prominent among countries with a history of non-interventionism. However, others saw Operation Alba as a necessary and justified response to the escalating security challenges and humanitarian crisis in Venezuela's border regions.

The role of the United Nations in Operation Alba played a crucial role in shaping international perception. The UN's endorsement and support lent credibility to the mission, alleviating concerns about unilateral intervention. The organization's involvement also facilitated cooperation and coordination among participating nations, enhancing the mission's effectiveness.

Media coverage of Operation Alba both domestically and internationally further influenced public opinion. While some outlets portrayed the mission as an essential intervention aimed at protecting vulnerable communities, others criticized it as an encroachment on Venezuela's sovereignty. The media's role in shaping public perception cannot be underestimated, as it significantly impacted the international community's understanding of the mission.

Non-governmental organizations (NGOs) also played a vital role in supporting Operation Alba, further shaping international perception. Humanitarian aid delivery was a central component of the mission, and NGOs played a crucial role in facilitating the distribution of essential supplies to affected communities. Their involvement highlighted the mission's humanitarian nature and garnered international support for Operation Alba.

Gender perspectives in peacekeeping operations in Venezuela's border regions also influenced international perception. The inclusion of gender considerations and the active participation of women in the mission challenged traditional notions of peacekeeping and highlighted the importance of gender equality in peace and security efforts.

Evaluating the effectiveness of Operation Alba in maintaining peace and stability was another factor that influenced international perception. As the mission progressed and tangible improvements became evident, support for the intervention grew among those who initially doubted its merits. The positive impact on Venezuelan communities and civilians further bolstered international support for Operation Alba.

In conclusion, international perception and reaction to Operation Alba were multifaceted and shaped by various factors. The role of the United Nations, media coverage, NGO involvement, gender perspectives, and the mission's effectiveness all played a crucial role in shaping how the international community viewed this historic peacekeeping mission. Understanding these perceptions and reactions is essential for historians and those interested in Operation Alba to gain a comprehensive understanding of the mission's global impact.

Conclusion: Lessons Learned and Future Implications for Multinational Cooperation in Peacekeeping Operations.

Conclusion: Lessons Learned and Future Implications for Multinational Cooperation in Peacekeeping Operations

The Operation Alba: Lessons from Operation Alba provides invaluable insights into the complexities and challenges of multinational cooperation in peacekeeping operations. This subchapter aims to summarize the key lessons learned from Operation Alba and explore their implications for the future of peacekeeping efforts.

One of the central lessons from Operation Alba is the critical role of the United Nations in fostering and coordinating multinational cooperation. The United Nations played a vital role in facilitating communication, establishing common goals, and coordinating resources among the participating nations. This experience underscores the importance of a strong and effective international organization in achieving successful outcomes in complex peacekeeping missions.

Another key lesson is the significance of addressing the security challenges and formulating effective strategies in conflict-prone regions like Venezuela's border areas. Operation Alba highlighted the need for a comprehensive approach that combines military efforts with diplomatic initiatives and humanitarian aid delivery. Multinational cooperation in peacekeeping operations requires a well-coordinated and integrated response to security challenges to ensure the safety and stability of the mission.

The impact of Operation Alba on Venezuelan communities and civilians cannot be overstated. The success of peacekeeping efforts depends on the support and cooperation of the local population. Operation Alba demonstrated the importance of engaging with communities, understanding their needs, and delivering effective humanitarian aid. Future peacekeeping missions should prioritize building trust and fostering positive relationships with local communities to achieve sustainable peace.

Operation Alba also shed light on the crucial role of non-governmental organizations (NGOs) in supporting peacekeeping operations. NGOs played a significant role in delivering humanitarian aid, providing essential services, and advocating for the rights of vulnerable populations. Their involvement highlights the need for closer collaboration between governmental and non-governmental actors in future peacekeeping endeavors.

Gender perspectives in peacekeeping operations emerged as another critical lesson from Operation Alba. Recognizing and addressing the specific needs and experiences of women and girls in conflict zones is essential for achieving lasting peace. Future peacekeeping missions should prioritize gender mainstreaming and ensure the meaningful participation of women in decision-making processes.

Evaluating the effectiveness of Operation Alba in maintaining peace and stability is vital for improving future peacekeeping efforts. Lessons learned from this mission can inform the development of best practices and strategies for future multinational peacekeeping operations.

Finally, media coverage and public opinion of Operation Alba played a significant role in shaping the mission's narrative and international support. Future peacekeeping missions should prioritize proactive and transparent communication strategies to ensure accurate and balanced media coverage, as well as foster public support for peacekeeping efforts.

In conclusion, Operation Alba provides valuable insights into the complexities and challenges of multinational cooperation in peacekeeping operations. The lessons learned from this mission have far-reaching implications for the future of peacekeeping efforts. By prioritizing effective communication, addressing security challenges, engaging with local communities, collaborating with NGOs, incorporating gender perspectives, evaluating effectiveness, and managing media coverage, future multinational peacekeeping operations can strive towards achieving sustainable peace and stability in conflict-affected regions.

www.ingramcontent.com/pod-product-compliance
Lightning Source LLC
Chambersburg PA
CBHW051305160726
47994CB00003B/1324